Hatchery of Tongues

HATCHERY

of

TONGUES

MICHAEL BASSETT

Negative Capability **PRESS**
MOBILE· ALABAMA

Hatchery of Tongues

Copyright © 2014, Michael Bassett

Cover and Interior Design by Ngim Tang
Edited by Karie Fugett

ISBN 978-0-9425-4496-1
Library of Congress Control Number: 2014937567

Negative Capability Press
62 Ridgelawn Drive East
Mobile, Alabama 36608
(251) 591-2922

www.negativecapabilitypress.org
facebook.com/negativecapabilitypress

*For Helen, my unexpected joy and
the inspiration for all my better voices.*

TABLE OF CONTENTS

IV. METAMORPHOSIS

ACKNOWLEDGEMENTS

I. BROOD STOCK

Bestiary for My Many Tongues

I have a hatchery of tongues, host
of tongues, harem of tongues. Some
of my childhood tongues have been knotted
like cherry stems, by little girls.
Some have no memory, only
longing for the lick
of something wet and electric.

Others are celibate and contemplative, hung
like drying tobacco in dark barns. Experimental
tongues have traded in their taste buds
for abstract expressionism. They know
what a lemon really is.

A coven of tongues bristle
like instruments on the dentist's tray,
sting the roof of my mouth
with their prayers.

The philosophical tongue, troubled
that it has no bone, yearns for the proof
of scalding coffee and persuasive
teeth. I couldn't say how many
of my tongues hum contentedly.

They all need thinking about.
Some need to be warned and watched:
the fop, the renegade, the fatuous drunk,
who means to get the job
done and come straight home
but always ends up slurring.

And there are those with mysterious
allegiances. Secretive,
they slither in private mythologies,
moving only when I sleep.

Deep Blue Awakenings

A woman sticking her finger into an aquarium
watches it turn into a goldfish. Her
plunging fist scuttles off
as a blue crab; her arm, up to the elbow,
an electric eel.

She is a mermaid, deathless blue,
back-floating, old tiara,
and string of pearls.

She thinks about the bathtub
with its cracks and stains.
Thinks about the sound
of running water, her husband's voice.

She saunters up the stairs. But the tub
has burst through the plaster
and waddles down Main
on iron feet, chasing
a wet dream all its own.

Something About the Way She Touches

I'm watching the way she coaxes
him into hitting her again.
It is an intimate thing,
ritualistic, like my mother burying
a burnt turkey in the snow.
Something about the way she touches
the tip of her tongue to her bloody lip
about the way his hand, red and hovering
somewhere between striking and reaching out
reminds me of being a boy
in the backyard at twilight, waiting
for the wind to make something beautiful
from the tears of pear trees.

Us and Them

Her hair on my pillow is the peace I'd get as a kid coming in from the ocean to the snoring air conditioning and the smells of coconut and perch cooking. I want to write a poem for the tenderness I feel for her knee socks, but instead I dream a solitary kestrel turns into a pale winter sun and finally into my father's face, bearded in foam and steam. No matter how I keep his head submerged under my beet-colored resentment, I'll always be in his study full of books too difficult for me. The past should be more pliant. I hope, here in this bed, she and I are parentless, not caring about the legacies that crawl like Escher lizards along a Möbius. But she may be lost in pills fetched for her mother. She may be dreaming of her daddy's flannel shirts and her opening bedroom door, the wand of light that doesn't reach.

The Blackboard of His Eyelid

He's a Chihuahua-eyed chicken boy
with hundreds of freckles
his mother swears are seeds
from the pumpkin they carved
him out of. But he knows where
babies come from. He knows the darkness
of the closet, where he listens
to his mother's crying. He learns, under
the henhouse, the weasel's way.

If he had Becky Wilson here,
he'd make her confess that she had lied
about how his parents make him drink
from the toilet and sleep
in a rabbit cage. A pale and skinny
clump of literature, always out past
the curfew of acceptance, behind
enemy lines of imagination, he plays
torturer of the inquisition,
brandishing the garden shears.

On the playground, while he practices
impossible contortions
of introspection, they bloody his nose,
hating the secrets hidden
in the scriptorium of his oddness.
They crack his sharp ribs, desperate
for the futures he reads
on the blackboard of his eyelid.
They shake from his green satchel
two dung beetles, most of a Mabel
Garden Spider, a scab from his skinned
knee, a sliver of bailing wire,
a cat's eye marble, and a quart
of Quick Start lighter fluid.

He can't stop thinking about apricots
shriveling, paint belching, tiny frogs
dripping above matches. Outside his secret
fort, sycamores yellow and crackle.

Occasional Fire

What's a man but a match, a little stick to start a fire?

— Miller Williams

It is not so hard to start a fire without a spark.
Spontaneous combustion happens.
Only sometimes the head is so cold.
The way a crumpled bumper's malevolent grin
will make you drive punctiliously for a while.
The way some folks scan the obituaries for anyone
younger than themselves and are briefly hollow,
though when they are discussed, most have not died
but relinquished earthly life or retired to eternal rest. This last
phrase makes you think of liberated circus elephants
painting abstracts in blood orange groves.
On my deck I discover the little brown corpse
of a salamander streaked like clay hillsides after a rainstorm.
Its snipped stub of a tail causes me instinctively
to touch my coccyx and think about evolution
and culture, the stultifying hokey pokey of history.

I look up at the bone meal sky and wonder
what do we know worth knowing
that Sophocles did not know?

What the crab nebula looks like?
The holy mysteries of the internal combustion engine?
The small sacrament of the PB&J?
That in language there are only differences?
The dangers of UV rays and free radicals?
The satisfaction of snapping off talk radio pundits,
superiority and indignation spreading
like whiskey glow in the gut?
Okay, eyeliner and curling irons go back to ancient times.
What about microwavable burritos?

Believing craftsmanship can mend passion
is like doctoring a sucking chest wound

with a really fine socket wrench.
So Vivaldi's Concerto No. 2,
lattice-worked sunlight, and dogwood blossoms can go flat.
All you need are a few good lines. Frank O'Hara's
"And as for the tire I never / even liked the wheel."

On the news it is all school shootings, delayed
disaster relief and failed disarmament. And a friend calls
to say she lost her house in the fire, and a friend calls
to say she lost her daughter in the fire.
Against so much suffering, how do you measure
the ghostliness of postindustrial man
or my ordinary loneliness?

You feel like a headless rooster crowing
with its feet. Instinct, convulsing habit, graceless need,
pure electric will. This is how so many keep going—
lonely as mountain gods, one-armed picadors,
wounded jesters—yes.

Yet there are moments. All that is required is your fingers walking
the creek bed of the spine of someone you love
lying beside you, conspiring over a crossword clue:
1. Down, four letters, Tin-can Eater.

All it takes is a change natural and inevitable
as tiny orange and red fish skeletons swimming
in the leaves of late summer trees.
Pumpkin, rust and ocher flickers.
Burn baby, burn baby burn.

MTV Turns 30

"Ladies and gentleman, rock and roll"
and a triumph of marketing disguised
as a cultural revolution.
"Video Killed the Radio Star" turned out
to be prophetic but not the whole story.
Some stars couldn't transition, as unfit
for the new medium as Clara Bow for talkies.
My adolescent dreams are filled with those Dada videos
like the Cabaret Voltaire exploding in a fisheye lens.
There is Rick Ocasec, a supermodel-dating wraith,
Rocking against a backdrop of morphing Hans Arpesque figures.
There too is Devo like nothing else from Ohio, too cool for sleeves,
anthropomorphic sprinkler heads,
a S&M Tupperware sideshow
come to HeeHaw land.

VJs were a new classification of humanity,
and there was Michael Jackson
wearing the moon's lost white glove.
And there, with his Buddy Holly glasses, gap teeth,
and fruity drinks, was Elvis Costello inexplicably jamming
in front of palm trees. There was Madonna,
like a virgin, with her wedding dress and lion,
beauty and her beast, ambition in a fishnet jersey,
Lilith of the new neon jungle.

In 11th grade American Literature, Redford's Gatsby
kissed Farrow's Daisy on the nose and Ms. Sabo asked
if we boys were taking notes. And I was,
but not like I had earlier studied the ecstatic reaction
produced by Duran Duran. I watched their videos
like a neophyte bank robber puzzling over schematics
he will never understand.

Remote Control gave us Colin Quinn
and Adam Sandler, while Ken Ober forged
in the smithy of his basement the collective unconscious
of suburban youth hoping for cool geekiness.

Coverage of *Spring Break* featured endless
rolling dunes of bronzed bodies
as lively as stock footage of 60's youth rallies,
but united not for peace and love
but for buff, a flexing bouncing proof theorem
for the democratization of beauty.

Like the loner in the train station sure that with all such
departures and arrivals there must be some happy
endings amidst all the décolletage and hard rock abs,
it was impossible to imagine sexual failure
or a pasty body. One even felt that all those hedonists
in Bret Easton Ellis novels would be okay.

Yo! MTV Raps fed slang into the vernacular quicker
than any beatnik, hep cat, or daddy-o ever split to antsville
to spread some long green and let the boogie woogie roll.

Beavis and Butthead broke Ehrenreich's assertion
about TV characters not being depicted for long stretches
watching TV and turned "uh huh huh huh"
moronic laughter into ersatz satire.

"The Real World" codified the plausibility
of reality television and engendered the current state
of affairs that purists and Nick-at-Niters
lament the way some classicists mourn
the burning of Alexandria.

MTV2 launched uninterrupted videos to show
the cyclical nature of trends, diversification
as undying as movie monsters from drive-in creature features,
whose fans must surely have thought
of them as inexhaustible.

Happy birthday eclectic montage maker.
Happy birthday purveyor of Iron Maiden, Run DMC, and U2,
champion of The Go-Go's, ZZ Top, and Depeche Mode.

Happy Birthday slicer, dicer, reifier of David Bowe,
Pet Shop Boys, Twisted Sister, keeper
of our Heart and The Police.
You're still young enough to party.

On the news today, there's a story
about Metalheads in Batswana, but on MTV
it's all *Teen Wolf* and gym tan laundry
on *The Jersey Shore*. Some little sociology professor
at the blackboard behind my eyes wants to say
that the whole saga is just a gateway drug
in the history of a culture's addiction to image.
But I still want my MTV and its marriage of power chords
and electric cave drawings. Its quick-cut-editing-desire
as valid as any. A striving, a generation reaching out
to plant our logo flag on the moon of wonder.

Close your eyes. There is Peter Gabriel wanting
to be your sledgehammer, his bad haircuts shifting
as he crescendos the rollercoaster tracks,
claymation bumper cars kissing his cheeks,
the ultimate expression of metaphor:
nothing contained, nothing staying itself.

Believe It

For heaven's sake, my dear, stop
flirting with that guy in the library.
My Love has read the Harvard Classics.
My Love is a captain in the crow's nest.
It sees with thousand-faceted-insect eyes,
always watching out for doom,
pretending to be moonlight caught in icicles,
always disguising its blood as sunset on the rocks.
Some say Happiness is the China Shop and Love the bull.
I say love begins with metaphors
flocking like birds to a garden statue.
My love has been them all: wild rose, master key,
guiding star, runaway truck, dirty street,
tulip farm in a leper colony, poetry-pockmarked moon.
My Love is on the waiting list at Johns Hopkins
for surgery that will remove all clichés.
My Love is a heart bleeding in a thorn bush.
You don't need that kick boxer.
My Love has a triple black belt.
My Love pillages with barbarian hordes.
My Love hang-glides at night.
My Love still needs a Donald Duck nightlight.
My Love likes to fall asleep reading
and then dream about all the characters.
It runs from shadows, but because it runs,
shadows know it is not one of them.
Shadows believe in My Love. Ancient Phoenician sailors
believe in the navigational accuracy of My Love.
Shy clerks leading double lives, wild-eyed artists,
exhausted workers in the canneries,
seven-fingered madmen and near-crippled saints,
even the most skeptical disciples of David Hume,
all believe in my Love. My Love knows that you
would never really start an environmentalist movement
where you call the Earth Mrs. Milky Eye Marble of Sorrow.
You love this blue crime planet. My Love sees
into that place in your soul
that is as blue as dragonfly wings,

knows the doubts you worry like a loose tooth,
the names of power and weeping nestled in your ear.
You believe that every plucky bubble you blow
must be its own little lucky world,
with before and after contained in now.
So why not believe in my Love?

Slugs

Sometimes when I sit on a bench and watch people strolling by, I think this one will die of congestive heart failure, that one will blacken in a mattress fire, this young mother will end tripping on a toy ninja, that cop choking on a peppermint stick. When I was eleven, neighborhood boys and I would gather slugs from our mothers' gardens. They were vaguely beautiful like the inside of clam shells, sunlight in gasoline, a cobalt and ash flake sky reflected in water. We'd meet at the lake with our mason jars and float out a wriggling pile on a piece of plywood. Before long, the birds would come. We'd stare at the diving beaks picking slugs off one by one. Some, dislodged by the commotion, fell or, as we liked to think, drowned themselves, desperate with horror. Rachel Smoke was the most voluptuous of the three Smoke sisters. After we had scraped up the $20, she sprinkled salt in her mouth, cupped a fat slug in her palm, then slowly dragged it across the edge of her bright pink tongue.

Now that, we moaned, would be the way to go.

Itinerant Face

My face makes plans
to visit every town named Normal
and creates a collection schedule
for dentures lost at amusement parks.

My face travels as a burlap sack; it believes
in what grows wild. It experiments
with sullenness like a toad that's done
with being teased. In it, moments sew themselves
up like change in a miser's coat.

In the bookstore, I ask my face why
it isn't smiling. "I thought you'd enjoy
Masks From Around The World," I say.
It's clearly more interested in
The History and Future of Amputation.
But it's learning to accept its fate, to lay itself
out like the shirt mother wanted me to wear.

When blind fingers come stroking for the silver
lining in every bone, my face is a door,
not the door of perception that once
I pass through I can never go back.
No, the other door.

Toad Man

You will suspect the shadows of his trousers. The words solitary beast never seemed less funny. But don't ask Toad for his story. He doesn't want yours, though he will listen if listening means staring at the welts on his flipper hands. With sad professorial eyes, he will weep for lost gypsy dancers burning red and purple.

Hunch in the trash-gray behind Delluchi's. Tell him a joke about crows and snow. Toad will retch muddy water, snot ballooning in his lime-flecked face. Buy a few origami cowboys and he will write you a riddle on a soup bone. A sip of Old Duke and he'll swear oblivion is owl screeches or the scalloped worm of the spine, the shy keyhole and the dark mouth.

Clairvoyant

We had to guess at the contents
of the bag she carried. Perhaps
shrouded in tissue the shrunken head
of the chess-playing lobster boy,
a ram's brooding tongue that told the hour
of your death, a five-pointed amulet
trapping women who smiled too much.

We knew the old woman had been a carnival
fortuneteller. She'd squeeze my elbow too hard
turning my small palm over. Children must
be shielded, she said, from the gaze of the Hollow Man.

I worried she knew about the drawings
in the shoe box under my bed
and what we did to Barbie in the shallow
pit out behind the Thompson place.
When I dream of her it is in a city
where all the windows have cataracts.

II. SPAWNING

Public Service Announcement from Desire

Everywhere people are diving
out of the sky, tracing
their genealogies, having their faces lifted,
earnestly bowling, ironic-nostalgia-bowling,
frozen turkey bowling, back floating
through afternoon sex, taking lavender baths, shaking
hands, meeting for designer coffee, licking
ice cream cones and peachy backs of knees.

No more kvetching about there being nothing to do.
Your soul's warrantee incites ardor, truly. Your shadow,
you must know, is solid gold.

Hurry through all the days of your necktie trying
its best to be a gibbet, through all the rhetoric of opportunity,
all the T.V. hours and unemployment weeks
of side-walk cafes and newsstand streets,
waiting for Springsteen's run away American dream
and Army ads claiming your real life adventure can begin.

If you'd rather, make the neo beat scene, get out
on the road and play at being the new Cassidy or Kerouac.

Maybe you just need to visit with Das Volk,
see a little bit of the country.
Go handle snakes in Appalachia.
Head down to Savannah and eat Jamaican food
on River Street, listen to root doctors
and the widowed librarians, sit on the park benches with tourist
gawking at manicured eccentricity.

Write bohemian kitsch in Key Largo, make pottery
in Montpelier, raise chickens and grow tomatoes
in Troy, Maine, find out why Normal, Illinois
probably isn't, take up with someone
you meet at the pavilion in Myrtle Beach.
Eat chili dogs and ride the Ferris wheel.
Feel tortured, if you must, but consider souvenir shop Americana,
stuffed space monkeys, celebrity bobbleheads, pecan logs,
and baseball caps ranged in their stoic phalanxes.

Why are your thoughts so glum?

These walls, walls of my perky self that my self
comes up against, could be any walls
where prisoners scrawl in the blood of their dying
hope, begging Godot to just knock
it off and show up already, begging their spirits
to rise like the Great Pumpkin never does
in the Charlie Brown Special, imploring
their futures to unwrap themselves
and find not emptiness but space.

Seriously, no more fingertip feathering
the bright purple bruises of your past.

Frank Capra saw idyllic America. New Age
Physicists saw Shiva Nataraj at the beach
in a Versace swimsuit of photons and destruction.

Your eyes are not the dead eyes of Monday motorist.
Your eyes are not hard, little porcupine eyes. Do you see
there are so many days that have not yet broken?
See the stunted boy contemplating his tall reflection
in a bottle shard, the two birds in the bush discussing
the philosophy of actualization, the countless suns waiting
like eggs yolks in the dark, dancing on the tip of a pin,
an infinity of angels listening for the next big bang.

Listen, the spoon may yet taste the soup.
The stones of the earth may finally sing
a new bloody song, as factories release millions
of silk purses newly minted from sow's ears.

Persist! Persist! Persist!

Hunt me. Hold me. Kiss me.
Catch me if you can.

The last word is never spoken. It winks
through branches, forward-scouting light
from a star not yet discovered.

Ubiquitous Witch Parable

A dark snake of lagoon water swallows
a scarf of moonlight orange as poison
arrow frogs. Moths hover like pale
faces of little girls. Every time
some hope is cheated, lightning bugs
flicker green. These senses
are so unreliable, hitchhikers
in the night.

Still we cork our thoughts like a jar of wasps,
certain somewhere there are songs
without teeth, where beauty is the easy
ventriloquism that bears up the night.
The coming morning is not even a dream
swimming under the skin
of the moon.

Another group is going down
to her candy cottage. Ceramic
knives sing songs from the womb,
while she sugarcoats the bitter pill. Desire
is not a riddle tied in knots
of wind. Like the collar-choked
cormorant, it dives for what's wriggling,
unmindful of what follows.

The First Date of the Razor Eater
and the Snake Charmer

She almost always hears the brutal music of her father's voice. His silence is an elegantly veiled threat, slithering like light under the closet door. Only when she performs does the quiet shed its desiccated skin. She wishes her desires were more brittle, like bones in canned salmon. But what she says is, " Posing akimbo, head thrown back, gulping abandon, that's for fools. You've got to place life and death flat on your tongue, sculpt your cheeks to the edges.

"No. No. No," he replies, swallowing her puckered fingers in his quick hand. "The cobra's hood is down, slick cable connecting nothing. The rattler's tail is still. The white that gives the cottonmouth its name remains unseen. The gaboon viper is a lustrous, turquoise-tinged bracelet."

All through pie and coffee, she watches the Red Man pinball machine go yellow and green and purple like a bruise in reverse. Little minnows swim in her wrists. He keeps biting back his words. She can't stop thinking about reaching into wire cages.

Ecce Puer

The little wizard tries on mother's rings
and cuts holes in her stockings
to make his masks. The four-eyed alchemist
mixes cooking sherry, turpentine,
and mud into potions that will turn
termites into giant-sized minions.

He will never outgrow
the starship captain, clutching
the throttle of father's bendable
reading lamp, exploring his study
full of secrets like those whispered
from another room at the edge of sleep.

Many worlds that were not
come to pass. Contemplate
the truths of science fiction.
Star Trek's Mr. Spock admires
Godzilla because they are both
half-breeds and improbably lovable.
Every image of otherness finds
humanity in some alien scene.

And so, Robbie the Robot
reads *The Sorrows of Young Werther*
and peeks into the holodeck
to watch a cozy family
of pointed-eared logicians play
multi-dimensional chess by the fire.

Our boy hero knows nothing
so readily found can be durable.
The spaceman may rescue
the Federation Princess only to learn
she is a changeling spy. Anything
may become something else.
But there is a point past which
metamorphosis cannot be reversed,
the sinister cocoon cannot be removed,
the mind control power of the Atomic Brain
cannot be undone.

Thales of Miletus and Tarzan's Jane

The Master of Adventure, the Jewels of Opar,
Leering Lizard Men: Is there no unity in these
phrases? No perversity in the tempted animal?

To ask is to flail at swarms of crazy wrists.
Forget peonies and the taste of plum sauce.
Use fussbudget as a safety word.

Still think you are the root of a conjugated verb?
Does the lantern flame shimmer? Wind stream?
Why trace tributaries along forearm or leaf?

No, the long and open use of the next far vine.
Match tips dark and occasional as bruises.
Origins are the only truly shocking things.

Will our hero or the crocodile emerge from the
underwater ballet? Is the imagination prisoner
or drum that we should beat it with sticks?

Cheetah will fetch help before the python
reaches the still stunned form. In a game of
bones, moonlight has oh so many bodies.

Do the jaws of insects eat all silence? Who
has put a jungle where my head should be?
Why instead of a head do I have the night sky?

Your fear is punctuated by end-stopped ellipses.
Transformations are not too dirigible. Learn
to forget your father's Geiger counter necktie.

Do people who like no one else doubly prove the
importance of sleep? Man or beast, will you hide
me in your eye? Have we always been together?

I would give up all metaphors for one word
to describe the dead carpenter clutching his saw.

Coyote And Eagle Visit
The Land of The Dead

In the days of the animal people,
when death was not
man's permanent portion
or constant cup,
the departed returned
in the spring, persistent
as resurrection fern,
seasonal as leaves.
But Eagle and Coyote
rooted around, beak and snout
in metaphysics. They journeyed
to the shadow land to swallow
the moon like an oyster
and spirit the spirits away.
But the past is swollen
with memories,
and Coyote's basket
could not hold the burden
of so many things
out of place. Stories,
no matter how many times
they're told, always go back
to the dark throat.
So people are cut down
and do not spring up.
And Coyote blows
and puffs his sadness
   at the laughing moon.

Belts

Wear one twisted
and it means you're
in love. Two twists
and you'll have twins or marry

a horse of a different color. At work
they're doomed like Atlas
to hold things up.
Tricky

the way they'll miss
a loop. In closets they hang
like drying snake skins, each
with a single tooth.

Crash Course in Phenomenology

Four yellow catfish in a mountain stream,
whiskered gods
frozen in an amber moment prove nothing,
mean everything.

In The Forest of Whispers

Bells with their stentorian tongues
cut out, hang as warnings
from branches laid
like fingers against
the divot above the upper
lip of sunset, where the red
wind makes the sound
of blood rushing through ears that come
alive with truth. Even the leaves seem
afraid of the forgetful mouths
of men. They remind us of notes
in trembling hands.

The Last Rope

-After Vasko Popa

Once a rope could amount to something.
Lure the little brown eel out of its cave.
Lariat the moon out of the Devils maw.
Taunt the most gluttonous smoke. Bully time:
"I'm going to divot the soles of your feet."

The last rope crawls between constellations.
At each fiery crossroads ties itself a knot
to remember what it could make of itself:
escapes, horizons, towers of death,
the plight of man stretched over the abyss.

III. BITTER SWEET SOUR SALTY

Alone on Interstate 95

Invigorating as a new piece of paper, I blink
and crayon stars scribble love notes:

Pirate Love Poem Written On A Napkin At The Holiday Inn

My longing wears your name
like an eye patch and a peg leg.
Love blows out the galley lanterns.
Love darkens the sky.
All I can see are the twin stars of your eyes.
The only lights I followed all winter.

Beckoning like anesthesia,
long-slept-on-dreams, nostalgia,
and loneliness squat

like exhausted hitchhikers
on the horizon. The night is unzipped,

the carcass of a raccoon. Black
trees amble along hunchbacked as a brood of trolls
heading into the mountains to escape
the argument between civilization and nature.

I see the moon as it must
have always been,
the eye of a beast
that suddenly thrusts its head
through your bathroom door.

Lights are semicolons
punctuating sentences
of danger. Desire
pierces my onion heart.

Waiting For Love to Make My Phone Explode

Most of my life is   waiting.
Waiting. For the acceptance letter to announce
my future's arrival at the banquet. Waiting.
For my nerve to get its sea legs.

Waiting. For the refund check, the meaningful silence,
the doctor to say turn and cough. Waiting.
To stop nodding like a funeral director.

Waiting   fills my mouth like a second tongue.
I am delinquent in all technologies.
Save waiting.
How many self-improvement books I ransack,
I am sullen and half-hearted in jobs,
hobbies, community service,
spirituality, and productive living.

No matter how often reason harangues
like a street preacher,
I keep lying in bed past noon.
Waiting for what I need
to stretch out and touch my thigh.

Essentials of Chance

*In the USA, the average number of people struck by lightning
is just under 100 a year. Ex-park ranger Roy C. Sullivan
(USA) was struck by lightning a world record seven times.*

Once he could think about other things,
scan *The Dictionary of Angels* and find
Seraphim were plentiful
as species of moths. Meanwhile,
his girlfriend sternly clipped
the islands of her toenails.
Her foot was a mystery he wanted
to explore in some bold Columbus way.

For a long time now he's jumped
at sundown's glint of light. He reads
weather reports like holy writ. The fulcrum
of reality phases in and out like a florescent bulb
in the throes of manic depression.

His eyebrows thin as new blisters remind him
he can't stay invisible. He knows
that rodents are not careless or less wise
than the talons of the dark. Nor is it generosity
that runs pink through their ringed tails.
Their dry skeletons are temples
to the essentials of chance.
Their broken-toe-keys
unlock the mysteries of bingo
halls and one-armed bandits.

So he gets a new job as a scarecrow
watching the horizon darken
like a wound congealing.

Goddess Next Door

She could change traffic
signals with mantras
and control the weather at will.

She could straighten
the spines of old ladies.
She convinced infants

to part with their tears,
made pears dance
to French folk-tunes,

and taught magpies charades.
The shrinks said
she was delusional.

But I think she knew
the cat's meow
before the electrodes.

Cassandra Syndrome

Heaven was on fire. The sky smoked
with a Pete's Cola advertisement.
My grandfather, a boy who had never seen
a skywriter, didn't wait to read the rest of the message.
He'd heard Reverend Quick preach many times on how
the world would PERISH in a wrath of fire.
So he took off like a hunted squirrel.
With his britches still unzipped,
he ran the three miles from Izora Brown
and her daddy's woodpile
to his own family's farmhouse,
where he couldn't get anyone to look.
His mama, mending a quilting loom, told him
to quit such foolishness. And older sister
Jessie said she would maybe come see later,
after the floors were swept.
No one believed his warning.
No one could see the writing
for the wall.

No telling how many yearnings

She's twisted like rooster necks. So many men with faces like skillets. Trouble, trouble, thats all she's been knowing, but Jodey is a good girl. She used to tell me, "Granny, you piloting a scarf of smoke and blood." She'd knock out a tooth, carve it into a little fish and wrap it in strands of black hair. She called darning needles devil's chatterboxes. She wanted to know how I got them to stop telling me secrets and why valentines are trimmed in flour sack and raccoon hide. She never was afraid of my gout, but fretted over ladders. She asked, "How can anybody trust such a long straight smile?"

A Case Study from the National Sleep Research Center

For Six Days Preceding His Death, No REM Sleep Could
Be Recorded In 33 Year Old Subject

His imagination scatters like roaches
under kitchen light. Nothing gathers
in the lugubrious street corners
of the mind. His was a fragment
from the text of war, a jot of shorthand
dictated by the voices of howitzers,
a hot metal flower cooling in his brain.

He saw x-rays everywhere: The tinted
windows of bank buildings, TV diner trays, glints
of sunlight on the rim without a net
at the courts behind the hospital.
But not in sleep. In sleep he no longer saw
anything. The petals of his mind closed,
his eyes still as stars.

In The Bones of His Hands, His Soul

He'd always been afraid
it would happen. Besides,

even if you weren't jumpy,
his was a shitty job: the cold

air writing threatening notes
in the bones of his hands, his soul

escaping in every blast
of breath.

He should have quit before
the steel door slammed behind him.

He never had any impulses
to just give up. With his 79 cent

lighter he burned meat labels
and melted cow fat. Trapped

in a purely human equation of waiting,
he wrapped himself in asbestos insulation.

It's not so different, he thinks,
from when David Kerr and the rest

of the Hellions locked him in his
Jr. High School locker. Just

keep your head, show you're brave
and the watching fates will be impressed

and help you find a way out. But
that hadn't been him in the locker. Delirious,

he had been with Kerr and the others, while Marvin
Buttons was caged in the locker.

Marvin, who wore the same dirty,
red sweatshirt everyday, with his long

hooked nose, and his girlish eyes always
looking down through wire rim glasses.

Getting sleepy now, he felt
the fluids in his body hardening,

a lazily droning airplane, frost buzzing
like a gnat at the corners of his eye.

His rescuers arrived after 72 hours,
a Guinness World Record. That

first night in the hospital he dreamed of horned
grotesques, born from sides of beef,

scuttling on broken and distended ribs.
In the middle of this orgy of meat twisted

in cubist violence, barely seen, like the visible
stinger of a wasp otherwise crawling with ants,

protruded the tip of a boy's nose
and the edge of wire framed glasses.

Light & Heavy

I do not know which is worse,
being a memory so hulking fat
your spindly bones are about to snap,
or an unstrung ghost puppet
with wild guesses for a backbone,
insecurity for a left shoe.

While blue siren lights played
over the abandoned tricycle next door,
the police talked to the man, whose
liver-spotted hands, triangular
as fish heads, shook so badly
he could hardly hold his cigarette.
I had heard the accusations, the shattering
plates of rage. I wondered if it was over
a VISA bill, some other lover, or was it just
the way people find each other by drawing blood.

"He lives alone. Poor crazy bastard.
Wife died years ago," a neighbor told me
while the dryers spun our double loads.

At the Northgate Stop

A cadaver got on the bus today,
wearing lions and yellowing lambs
snuggled in a dream of dirty clouds.
The zombie had beige tufts
of ear hair and colonies
of acne warring on his face.
Everyone tried to ignore him.
On a silver mouth harp,
he blew a few notes,
like hogs chewing snake heads
and sour figs at twilight.
Eyelids and newspapers fluttered.

Someone's infant started pointing
and crying so that the dead kid
rubbed the cigar burns on the
thinnest of arms and looked down
at the steel-bolted parasite climbing
his crippled leg, like he was noticing,
finally, a much beloved dog
that had just finished
squatting on a neighbor's rug.

The Whole Neighborhood

When CeCe Williams crept up
on her husband, the pastor
of our local congregation who had
had sexual congress with one of his flock
and fallen asleep on the couch
watching Johnny Carson,
she krazy-glued his hand
to his exhausted member.
Then she threw on all the lights,
put "Sympathy for the Devil"
on the stereo, and woke
the whole neighborhood
to teach us how hard
it is to let go
of what we love.

The Fall

Arms windmilling wildly, hands
grabbing as if to catch the ropes

of his own screams, he plunges
from the damaged plane, cursing

the thinness of air. But neither
the cigar breath of his jump instructor,

nor the mercy of heaven, nor yet the image
burrowing through his mind

of his mistress's cruel smile
could slow his insatiable descent.

From the corner of a watering eye
he watches the mountains growing

from jagged mint candy to an ocean
of white blindness. Even through the shock,

his nerves are insistent as hungry birds.
Wet and rancid and steaming

hot in the snow, he rolls down
until finally inertia and consciousness

let him go. In the hospital,
his sight dim, his hip shattered,

his spine broken like the axle of a toy wagon,
he is happy to tell the nurses his story

of cheating death until he falls again
into morphine dreams.

IV. METAMORPHOSIS

The Abridged Field Guide to Silences

Some silences teach us how to read shoes. Others you follow like pinpricks of firelight in a pig's eye. Some ask you to name the current President before the pages of history fall like crippled birds into a polar sea. Odd ones taste like caramel or thistles. White ones are janitors turning mop heads into schooners. One or two pluck curiosity and disgust off the back of your neck. Lingering ones hunch like forgotten gods, stitches in a smile rising in a polished spoon.

The Other Museum

In the Great Rotunda, the replica
of a train dreams of when it was a killer
whale that swallowed sinners.
"There is no graffiti" is spray-painted
on the side of a sleeping boxcar.
Lazarus, who resembles a salami sandwich
left under a car seat, buttonholes
every passing kid to warn them about
sunspots, fast food, riding lawnmowers.

In the Alcove of Unanswered Questions,
queries flop like dying fish.
Who was the first to taste teeth?
What do mirrors imagine in the dark?

In the Gallery of Insomnia,
Cain and his brother sell knives
to stab sleep. Dark mice nibble
the piping off pajamas, and
Ahab punches tickets
in the Wax Exhibition of Retired
Archetypes while Quixote leers
at a *Penthouse*. His automated
windmill charger galumphs
in and out of action.

Beneath the Arch of Failure,
Cupid convinces Phoenician sailors
to believe in the navigational
accuracy of Love,
then rides off with the Mongol Hordes.

In the Hall of Undiscovered Books,
a treatise hangs like winter
light in skim milk, trackless
as the blank page, a volume far
above you, the last moment
of a luckless diver.

Aphorisms of One Who Calls
Himself Legion Because He Is Many

When it comes to diatribes on depraved
Appetites, cold roast is often more indignant
than wormy apples.

Everything beautiful demands restitution
for the betrayal of metaphor.

The folded note is both tame as a gravy boat
and sexy as a pitchfork.

Need is desire in sensible shoes.
Regret, a dancer with a pet thorn in one slipper.

Logic is a narcissistic cockatrice.
Devils are branded gods
and gods are gilded devils.

There is an indecision that stands
paralyzed by possibility, like Cold War defectors
in the aisles of Super Saver Convenience Stores.

Some analogies argue about whether
they failed because of cheap grace or bad faith.

Some truths dream of a cat heaven
where there are perfect flea collars,
others of one where there are no fleas.

Some truths prefer the company
of crabgrass.

Some truths put on black berets
and false mustaches. Others hold
their breath till they are blue
as platypus bills.

Some poke out their eyes
with geraniums. Others curl up
with a golden cactus.
Some are broken-jawed pliers.
The rest are skinned nails.

The wounds we cannot live
without define us the way the night
sky outlines the stars.

The wounds are the stars
and the night the definition.

We are engaged with language.
Words are our only weapons.

People who live in glass houses
should wear mirrored clothes.

For every aphorism there is an equal
and opposite aphorism.

Directives

Grackles, scatter like pieces
of a story. Sweethearts
of ash and butter, finger
squint-star light, draw
a spine down the highway.

Tiers of time, pile rock.
Careless boy, search for a treasure
to replace mother's smashed geode.

Crippling moments, restless
as beach fleas, announce yourselves.
Cautious consumer, do not so easily
pass up Jack the Ripper's garters.

Moons, gossip like monkeys
anticipating things born
between the pull of tides.

Fleshy fruits, dream of a day
when the air will not be
a thousand different flutterings.

Death devolves
into a little girl plucking
fountain pennies.

Errata

For snake, read trust. For stick, understand poking
around in the anthill of time.

For walking, substitute sitting on the toilet
with your legs falling asleep when a woman crawls
out of the cabinet under the sink and gives you
a little doll of yourself.

For lonely nights, substitute Midas
admiring his pile of burnished apples.

For wizard, substitute the jilted chump
sending a nice wedding present.

For the story of the urchin raised by trolls,
read spending $29.99 on the latest edition
of *Seduction for Cretins*.

For the little trash-can-spider,
hanging on a string of spittle,
substitute a dark star falling
on a moonbeam.

For errors, substitute errors.
For eyes, substitute splinters.

Some of Mythology's Big Guns Answer the Questions of An Aging Newsstand Poet

Welcome, ancient fathers!
You know this thrumming
walk of humanity,
this slouching into commerce.
What does it mean?

Job: "There are no answers,
only snot-nosed brats
and more cattle to lose in their season."

Cronos: "With flint teeth,
I bit off my father's dick."

Utnapishtim: "Death can be nice."

Once I cast my blossoms
before the mandala of the womb,
prayed with my body
for the mysteries only art
can reveal. Why did I brave
goddesses with flailing octopus
hair, dark eye sockets
full of teeth, round hips
curving beyond horror?

Job: "Read romance novels. Fly a kite.
Eat potato salad."

In my youth I begged for the dark smile
of a mystical orifice, the significance of zero.
I fed on stale cheese kisses and danced
through seamless nights. What did it come to?

Cronos: "The dark, vein-webbed father cock,
my scepter of power. Can you dig it?"

I sought for truth to hike her dress
above her hips and let me have my few
strokes. Love came to me like a crocodile.
But my bones have softened in this lukewarm
blood. What happened to my passion?

Utnapishtim: "The same nagging family.
The same inescapable me, forever and forever."

I see death in the trees
flying off like shadows. People
spreading their cares on chili
dogs with little plastic wands.
Skid marks in the parking lot are burnt
corpses of horseshoe crabs.
Everyday it gets harder to see
my wife's face. I fear my sons
will never find me.

Cronos: "Bye-bye wiener."

Job: "Only daycare
and cattle farts."

Utnapishtim: "A one-minute egg."

Evening Parchment

A broken lounge chair, cracked shells,
a warped backdoor snuggling into its frame,
What are dreams but the love
of getting hurt? The dogs of hunger
nosing through trash? The prayers
of briars for the taste of skin?

All the guttural
sounds of desire, dusted
with death, measure the last
light's slow translation.
Dragonflies, making dusky love,
write the infinite
sadness of new beginnings
their bodies caught
in a flurry of parchment wings.

Evening In Early Winter

From the sleeves of your dark coat
woven out of silence, you dip your cold finger
into me, dial the number of my sadness.

Ash falls from the pockets of your eyes.
The pain shimmers like light on water.
It can't find a form that will suit it.

A giant grouper swallows every quick,
silver thought. The sleek, black, muscular spirits
circle, waiting for the coronation of their king.

There was a name I needed.
I had forgotten what is coming.
Now it is too late to believe.

What We Name

Something calls the mud wasp,
tattooed with death, back
to the fallen nest, broken
catacombs covered with snow,
nosed up by desperate dogs.

Whatever we name
chance or destiny is no more
or less than the hastening lights
that open the hearts of night
creatures to the moon.

Grocery List Manifesto

A nuthatch slides down the live oak head first.
The sun dissolves into pale salmon light,
lingering like my friends grocery list
stuck on the refrigerator. My mind
won't let it go. Under bread, eggs,
toilet paper, she'd written Forever Sunlight.
Maybe, Forever Sunlight is a brand
of detergent or shampoo, but this could be
her subconscious penning a cryptic wish.

Perhaps everybody has a secret word
in their grocery list, a Freudian wish, hunkering
like a fox waiting in the snow
behind rows of more obvious realities.
I am suddenly desperate to see Ellen Kieser's
frolicsome revelations hidden in her grocery lists.
She of the cotton-candy-pink streaked hair
I kissed at the sixth grade pool party
doing my best impression of Don Johnson.

How many people's secret word is just a name,
a name they could aerosol on a wall,
a name like an act of God in the nervous system,
that one name that spills its syllables
into every other sound. Maybe it slips
in between the contexts of other letters.
Think of the millions of lists, pretending
to be so prosaic, yet actually swimming
with the intricate vocabulary of desire.

Skeptical? The lesson I'm really getting
at is about becoming better decoders,
which means more skillful voyeurs.
Between the darting of eyes, the quick
pushing back of chairs, the hurried buttoning
of coats, the coughing into hands, and all
the countless gestures of embarrassment
and retreat, we must be careful
sneaking up on our own secrets.

New Standardized Test for Dementia

Identify a pencil by

      (A)   letting it become your eye
      (B)   asking a librarian
      (C)   stabbing it into a kneecap
      (D)   pencils died out about the same time
               as teeth marks and algebra

The current President of The United States is

      (A)   happily married to television
      (B)   one who steps on rubies thinking
               they are cockroaches
      (C)   the infinite emerging from approval ratings
               which you have denied
      (D)   a toaster with epaulets named satisfaction
               and accomplishment

Draw a clock face. Which of the following
does it most nearly resemble?

      (A)   a diary entry of no date
      (B)   a road sign for abiding
      (C)   a snake hole full of price tags
      (D)   the cartoon goose egg of the mind

Choices

Sometimes, because my father was well
into philosophy, we got lost. Other times,
my mother was calculating
the exact worse decision
in her married life. "Look,"
he would tell her, "we have all got to choose
between the world we see in our heads
and the world we see everyday."

I read about a woman who drank a mouthful of ants,
she hadn't, till too late, noticed in her dipper of well water.
So horrified by the thought of live ants inside her,
she drank insecticide that sent her convulsing.

Michael Golding, one of the older scouts,
always asked the new ones, would you rather
have your little finger or your little toe cut off.

Outside my window, warblers flit indecisively
through wax myrtle. The clock peels of its face.
Memory sleeps under my sea-of-blood
eyes blinking at the honeyed knife.

The dead woman counts the ant divots
on her swollen tongue. An angel
licks the tip of a pencil.

Dichotomy

Today I had to define the word
for my American Lit class, and in that instant, I
transformed into the forked tongue of a snake,
the paths in the black woods running
away like lies to meet each other,
the unfulfilled desire strangled
in Plato's gray-splotched beard,
the praxis bleeding
in the bathtub with Ockham's razor,
the knower and the known,
plotting in the dark, poking ice picks
at each other in the cloven dark.

Wishing

Old coins at the bottom of fountains
rub their noses off.
One wish leads to another.

Remember when you hoped
there might be some
loophole out of all

life's limits? Recall when you discovered
the perfect way to con
the lamp genie? I wished

puddles were invisible
on pants' legs, that Melissa Thomas would
check the Yes box, that I had

three more wishes. I wished that words
knew how to spell themselves
and Moby Dick could just be a whale.

Three more wishes. I wish I could see
Mrs. Woodyard, my Fifth Grade teacher, naked
and that I had never seen the beaches of Baja

at lent littered with severed
turtle heads. Give me more
whiskey courage, my dad less cancer.

I wish I could stop wishing.
All those birthdays I had to close
my eyes and pretend

because I was embarrassed
to stand there wavering
like a flame.

The Life and Times of My Last Idea

My last idea was convinced that time
had something allegorically to do
with birds. Clock hands are crippled wings.

My last idea was comforted that Einstein said
he only had one idea his whole life.

My last idea took classes in epistemology and baking.

A calloused stub of a finger, my last idea
never became the Emperor of Prodding
or even Assistant to Regional Poking.

My last idea was just another suicide,
not the bill of a transparent sailfish.

My last idea wanted a parting kiss.
Its tongue, a tiny red fox squirrel,
cavorted between its teeth.

My last idea fell out of context
like the henna colored roach
that dropped from the hole
in the ceiling of discovery.

Articles of Faith

Guilty pleasures are hard for the highbrow.
I prefer Eddie Rabitt's "I Love A Rainy Night"
to Niikuni's poem and visual essay on rain.
But, I won't always admit that my favorite movie
is the 1933 original *King Kong*
(even though it's on the Time Top 100 Films List).
Sometimes I say Cocteau's *Beauty and the Beast*
or *Lawrence of Arabia* or *My Dinner with Andre*.
Occasionally, I go another way.
Whimsy pushes its beak through the eggshell of better sense
and I blurt out *Ishtar*, knowing they'll never buy it.
Sometimes funny words describing funny things
(comiconomenclaturist)
are not as funny as more pedestrian syllables. "Frog."
Let your tongue leap from the lily pad. Say it,
frog, frog, frog, frog till you've gigged
all the meaning from the dark creek of language.
Sometimes the words for violent or pathetic realities
are funniest of all: defenestration, pilgarlic.
The orneriest mood can pass so quickly.
An enigmatic smile at the bus stop and the accursed
summer is scented with willows, rich with pulchritude,
purple butterflies and dragonflies on the wing.
Conversely, the sky is so blue you are forced
to contemplate the concept of authenticity.
Your morning seems set to a soundtrack: the opening strains
of "Sweet Jane" the Velvet Underground version,
a prelapsarian waterfall rippling electronic joy.
Then, one unguarded memory and you're playing
whack-a-mole with a hundred betrayals. The ski-lift
of regret leads to the disco palace of ghost wrestling.
All the advice you give or get becomes a pageant of paraders
with clichés stenciled across their chests.
Yes, even fantasies sour. Deal with it.
Time to throw out your murderous icicle,
get some air, fly a kite, take a bath.
Don't go to the art house theater with your friends
who are suspicious of mountain imagery and symbolism,

but beware of analogies about sailfishing
and metaphors based on mating hawks or industrial glue.
Don't send your exes snapshots of the sea.
The discovery that great whites enjoy the music of ACDC
gives me hope that there really was something primordial
and profound in the manic sexual havoc of the baselines
I played badly in my brother's garage speed metal band.
You cannot explain irony to the pigtailed girl
clutching a corndog, dancing with her beagle
at the bluegrass festival. Narrate your own leading scenes,
even if there is no real narrative, just the shaky rails
of time and the imagined point on the horizon.
Put away your half-finished puzzles. Go outside.
Make a New Year's resolution to teach
all the Macaws to squawk "party on."
Watch the poetry-pockmarked moon
scatter its silver confetti.

After Amputation

Each mistake unpronounceable
as a face with time's new
identification ticking arrow tongues.
Lips gelid as oysters
slurping all the phonetics
that substitute for sensation.
Because one selection leads
into another, the necessity
for learning seems urgent.
Each lost beginning sensitive
as a hand that endured
piano lessons, helped
undo bras, did the best
it could, matching
its life to yours.

Crowsfeet, Possumtail, and Moonwort

By the pond she doesn't remember legends about animals becoming plants when they die. But she does know some stories about the moon liking to play dress up. On the evening news we see an armless girl making veal parmesan with her feet and putting in contact lenses with a big toe. Later, watching spiders caught between the pane and screen of a window winter warped, I ask her what the moon is disguised as now. A fossil, she tells me. I think it was Kierkegaard who wrote, "I myself am a myth about myself." She stops me with a kiss. The baby octopus moon pretends to be a kite tangled in a leafless tree.

Asleep In the House of Being

I had just stolen Batgirl's silver
pancake makeup case and convinced
her to elope to the Sugar Bowl
when you interrupted me
to tell me your dream. You said,
"There's an ontological ambiguity
to a sewing needle: one end wanting to prick
the other blinding itself." I asked, "When
did your breasts become sea urchins?"
You heard something. So we climbed down
into a cellar to look for it. No light
except for the flashlight you dropped.
When you picked it up, I had vanished.

Under the folds of a problematic purple sky,
we climbed down into a bed
of dark mussels. You cut your foot.
And I kissed it. With a flash
of moon-lit eye, a startled heron
flew out over the waters.
Silence and some feathers.

ACKNOWLEDGMENTS

Thanks to the editors of the following publications where some of the poems in this collection have appeared:

Apostrophe: Aphorisms of One Who Calls Himself Legion Because He Is Many

Barrow Street: Something About the Way She Touches

The Cherry Blossom Review: Evening in Early Winter

Cider Press Review: Crash Course in Phenomenology and Crowsfeet, Possumtail and Moonwort

Coal City Review: In The Bones of His Hands, His Soul and Cassandra Syndrome

Concho River Review: Awakenings and The Whole Neighborhood

FUGUE: The Blackboard of His Eyelid

In The Yard: Evening Parchment

Iodine: Alone on Interstate 95

The Journal of College Writing; Occasional Fire and Articles of Faith

Kakalak: Clairvoyant

Lullwater Review: Wishing

POMPA: Bestiary For My Tongues and Belts

Rhino: No Telling How Many Yearnings

SAMSARA : Essentials of Chance

www.ingramcontent.com/pod-product-compliance
Lightning Source LLC
Chambersburg PA
CBHW022037090426
42741CB00007B/1107